Religion and Marxism

Religion and Marxism
An Introduction

Paul-François Tremlett

SHEFFIELD UK   BRISTOL CT

Published by Equinox Publishing Ltd
UK: Office 415, The Workstation, 15 Paternoster Row, Sheffield,
South Yorkshire S1 2BX
USA: ISD, 70 Enterprise Drive, Bristol, CT 06010

www.equinoxpub.com

First published 2023

© Paul-François Tremlett 2023

All rights reserved. No part of this publication may be reproduced or transmitted in any form or by any means, electronic or mechanical, including photocopying, recording or any information storage or retrieval system, without prior permission in writing from the publishers.

British Library Cataloguing-in-Publication Data

A catalogue record for this book is available from the British Library.

ISBN-13 978 1 80050 287 1 (paperback)
         978 1 80050 288 8 (ePDF)
         978 1 80050 352 6 (ePub)

Library of Congress Cataloging-in-Publication Data

Names: Tremlett, Paul-François, author.
Title: Religion and Marxism : an introduction / Paul-François Tremlett.
Description: Bristol, CT : Equinox Publishing Ltd, 2023. | Includes bibliographical references and index. | Summary: "This concise and accessible introduction brings the writings of Marx and Engels and later thinkers in the Marxist tradition including Althusser, Gramsci, the Frankfurt School as well as Liberation Theologians such as Gutierrez and Maduro, into focus in relation to questions of religion, social change and social justice"-- Provided by publisher.
Identifiers: LCCN 2022045134 (print) | LCCN 2022045135 (ebook) | ISBN 9781800502871 (paperback) | ISBN 9781800502888 (pdf) | ISBN 9781800503526 (epub)
Subjects: LCSH: Communism and religion.
Classification: LCC HX536 .T64 2023 (print) | LCC HX536 (ebook) | DDC 261.2/1--dc23/eng/20221230
LC record available at https://lccn.loc.gov/2022045134
LC ebook record available at https://lccn.loc.gov/2022045135

Typeset by S.J.I. Services, New Delhi, India

Contents

Preface   vii

1 Introducing Marx   1

2 Marx: Religion, Power, Ideology, and Change   10

3 Engels: The First Marxist Historian and Anthropologist of Religion   20

4 Hegemony, Ideology, and Religion: Althusser, Gramsci, and the Embrace of Uncertainty   31

5 The Frankfurt School: Horkheimer, Habermas, and Religion   42

6 Marxism and Liberation Theology	52
7 Conclusions	62
Glossary	65
References	69
About the Author	75
Index	76

Preface

The idea for this book emerged after working with Massolit's Samir Haroon to produce a video lecture series for A-Level sociology students on 'Marxism and Religion'. The book was written with the same kinds of students very much in mind. However, I have made substantial changes to the original Massolit lectures, including a new chapter on Engels as well as significant revisions to the chapters on Althusser and Gramsci and on liberation theology. I have also added new material on the figures of Auguste Comte, Edward B. Tylor, Max Weber, Sigmund Freud, and Donna Haraway, all of whom are important to sociology. Directing attention to the work of scholars situated outside the conventional marxist canon demonstrates the extent to which that canon is implicated in intellectual developments across a range of academic fields including history, sociology, anthropology, psychoanalysis and feminism. I have also referenced key sociological concepts including modernity, orientalism, secularization, functionalism, power, and lived religion to foreground the connections between Marx and Engels's thought and wider concepts and debates in the sociology of religions. It is hoped that these changes will also help to broaden the book's academic audience.

I have also sought to broaden the appeal of the book to a more general reader by representing Marxism (firmly with a capital M) not as a unitary, dogmatic or monolithic body of writing, belief and practice, but rather as a complex, contested and heterogeneous terrains of human thought and activity. There is significant diversity of thought and practice among marxists, from scientific (or messianic) marxism with its unshakeable conviction that history will deliver the promised land, to the marxism 'without guarantees' of Stuart Hall.

I have also resisted the temptation to represent Religion (very much with a capital R) as something fixed and monolithic, and to stereotype religious identities in terms of dogmatic adherence to institutionalised norms of textual interpretation

Preface

and social behaviour. To be sure, both Marx and Engels lived at a time when religions seem to have been understood and experienced in much this kind of way; Marx's family were Jews who converted to Christianity to evade anti-Semitic prejudice, while Engels's family were pious Protestants. Moreover, when Marx and Engels wrote about religions, they were primarily thinking of monotheism and Christianity, which effectively stand in for all the other religions and religious forms in their writings. But today we are better able to understand the diversity *of* religions (for example, Buddhism, Christianity, Hinduism, Islam, Judaism, Rastafarianism, and Scientology) and the diversity *within* religions (buddhisms, christianities, hinduisms, islams, judaisms, rastafarianisms and scientologies). Moreover, the interest among contemporary sociologists in lived religions – the everyday experiences of religious communities, groups and individuals – has opened out religions not as discrete containers filled with particular rules, beliefs, texts and institutions and so forth, but as porous intersections where wider cultural, political, and secular dispositions meet and combine. For example, contemporary British Muslims can simultaneously be pious, participate in Christmas, and work in secular environments such as hospitals, universities, and the emergency services. In short, like most British people today, British Muslim lives and identities blend religious and secular practices and comportments, enabling them to move seamlessly in and out of religious, secular, domestic, and workplace spaces. This important observation informs us that religious lives are lived out not at the mercy of overpowering religious institutions or according to the inflexible interpretations of religious texts but are moments at which multiple ideas and practices converge and combine.

It is often forgotten that the words 'communism' and 'socialism' were not invented by Marx and Engels and not conceived in opposition to religions. In fact, the terms emerged in France, in the early part of the nineteenth century, among followers of Henri Saint-Simon (1760–1825), amidst intense debates about what form post-revolutionary French society should take. In 1789 on the eve of the French Revolution, the alliance of Church, aristocracy, and monarchy stood opposed to progressive change but by 1830, religion was no longer opposed to revolution. Indeed, for a short time it was its ideological foundation, as various figures came forward to argue that the Gospels actually provided the moral basis for a new society. Among others, Louis Blanc (1811–1882), Philippe-Joseph-Benjamin Buchez (1796–1865), Étienne Cabet (1788–1856), Charles Fourier (1772–1837), Victor Hennequin (1816–1854) and Felicité Lamennais (1782–1854) made the case for a new Christianity, freed from what appeared then to be the dead weight of the Church, that would provide the social cement for post-revolutionary French society. Buchez founded the newspaper *L'Atelier* in 1840 and called for the 'working class to draw on the moral values of early Christianity – that is, on the original teachings of Christ, before his message was perverted by the established Church' (Berenson, 1984: 43). Cabet, the leader of the Icarians who would go on to establish religio-socialist communes in the United States, argued in 1846 that *'Le christianisme c'est la fraternité, c'est la communisme'* ['Christianity is fraternity, it is communism'] (quoted in Pilbeam 2000: 499). In 1843 Hennequin, writing in the Fourierist newspaper *Démocratie pacifique* declared, *'Deux puissances existe: l'esprit moderne et la foi catholique; on ne peut pas les détruire: il faut donc les unir'* ['Two powers exist: the modern ethos and the Catholic faith: they cannot be destroyed, so they must be united'] (quoted in Pilbeam, 2000: 505).

The overriding message of this book is that marxisms and religions can be sites for sincere debate and critical reflection on our histories and experiences rather than occasions for disinformation, polarisation and intolerance. It is my hope that this book contributes in some small way to that end.

Chapter One

Introducing Marx

Why study Marx? Marx was a nineteenth-century thinker trying to understand the economy and society of his day. He is perhaps most well-known for writing, with his friend and collaborator Friedrich Engels, the political tract *The Communist Manifesto*. However, he also developed an original theoretical model for analysing processes of social, political, economic, and indeed religious change, and this model has been extremely influential in the academic fields of history, sociology, and anthropology, including French, Italian and

German social theory as well as theology. We will begin by exploring the intellectual context in which his ideas emerged before moving on to consider them in greater detail. But before we do that, just how did Marx conceive of religions? What position do they occupy in his theory of society and processes of change?

> Modernity is arguably *the* organising concept of sociology, and around it cluster a range of theories of religious as well as economic, political, and social change. In classical sociological accounts of modernity, increasing freedom and prosperity is accompanied by the loss of religious and cultural values and the breakdown of traditional communities, to be replaced by self-interest, egoistic calculation, and *anomie*. One of the most quoted sections from *The Communist Manifesto* is Marx and Engels's description of modernity – what they called the 'bourgeois epoch' – in terms of 'constant revolutionising of production, uninterrupted disturbance of all social conditions, everlasting uncertainty and agitation . . . All fixed, fast-frozen relations, with their train of ancient and venerable prejudices and opinions are swept away, all new-formed ones become antiquated before they can ossify. All that is solid melts into air' (Marx and Engels 1967: 83).

Introducing Marx

A number of critics of Marx's approach to religions argue that he reduces them to little more than the epiphenomenal effects of economic and social processes. As such they accuse him of reductionism which means, rather than engaging with religions, he explains them away as the products of social and economic processes.
Yet Marx's approach to the study of religions is important because, even if at first sight his approach appears directed towards explaining religions away, he nevertheless reminds us that religions are implicated in social and economic relations and therefore, to understand religions we need to include these important layers of context. Furthermore, given Marx's interest in elites, his approach also reminds us of the importance of power in the study of religions, from the power of seemingly untouchable religious institutions to the study of religious minorities struggling for a voice.

Marx was born in 1818 in Trier, which today is in Germany close to the border with Luxembourg. He was born into a Jewish family – his father was a lawyer who converted to Christianity to evade anti-Semitic prejudice. The young Marx studied law at the University of Bonn and then at the University of Berlin, before switching his studies to philosophy, having fallen under the influence of a group of thinkers known as the Young Hegelians. He completed his doctorate on the ancient Greek philosopher Democritus in 1841.

Religion and Marxism

Marx had hoped to pursue an academic career, but his radical views led him to journalism, and he wrote for and edited a number of radical newspapers in Germany, France, and Belgium. In 1844 in Paris, he began a lifelong collaboration with Friedrich Engels. Together they wrote *The German Ideology* in 1846, although it wasn't published until 1932, long after both had died, and *The Communist Manifesto*, which was published in 1848. Marx's political activities eventually forced him into exile in London, where he remained with his wife and children until his death in 1883. Throughout his time in London Marx wrote prodigiously, notably the *Contribution to a Critique of Political Economy*, which was published in 1859, and volume I of *Capital*, which was published in 1867, as well as numerous reports, articles and letters. Two further incomplete volumes of *Capital* were edited and published by Engels in 1885 and 1894 respectively.

From this brief sketch of Marx's life two observations that have been made by a number of commentators are worth highlighting: the first concerns the influence on Marx's thought of the German philosopher Hegel and of the Young Hegelians, a group of theologians and philosophers including Ludwig Feuerbach among others, particularly on his early writings. The second addresses the suggestion that Marx's ideas turned away from the language of German

Introducing Marx

philosophy around 1845. We will take each of these observations in turn.

Georg Wilfred Friedrich Hegel was born in Stuttgart in present day Germany, in 1770. His ideas were shaped by the events of his time, particularly by the French Revolution in 1789. One of his most important books was his *Lectures on the Philosophy of History* in which he argued that 'the History of the world is none other than the progress of the consciousness of Freedom' (1914: 19–20). Hegel conceived of world history as a unified, rational process. Beginning his account with the ancient Chinese, Indian, and Persian empires, Hegel argued that these were 'stationary' civilizations where only the ruler was free. He then turned to the ancient Greeks. There a concept of freedom had emerged, but the Greek society of the time depended on the institution of slavery, so only some could be free. But with the Reformation in sixteenth-century Europe a new culture had broken through that regarded the individual as a rational agent responsible for its own salvation. Later the spirit of the French Revolution would promise to shine Enlightenment reason on every corner of government and culture, in what Hegel described as a 'glorious mental dawn'. For Hegel, then, a new kind of rational, free community had emerged on the global stage.

Religion and Marxism

Hegel's model of world history has Europe at its centre, with freedom radiating outwards to encompass the entire globe. His model is not simply Eurocentric but reproduces prejudices about the superiority of white cultures over 'stationary' others and is an example of what Edward Said called 'orientalism'. According to Said, orientalism is founded upon 'an ontological and epistemological distinction between the Orient and . . . the Occident' (Said 1979: 2). Notably, Marx's scattered references to 'Asiatic despotism' and the 'Asiatic . . . mode of production' are steeped in the same white, orientalising, Eurocentrism. As Bhambra has argued, any 'model that posits a world-historical centre from which developments diffuse outwards is problematic' (Bhambra 2011: 673). She argues that conventional accounts of modernity have tended to deny its implication in colonialism and the extraction of materials – from human bodies (slaves) to rubber and sugar – from Africa, Asia and the New World. According to Bhambra, modernity was not a process endogenous to Europe, but emerged out of asymmetric encounters with non-Western societies.

Introducing Marx

The idea that history was a journey which would conclude with the founding of a new political community appealed to Marx. But it was also Hegel's application of 'dialectic logic' to the study of history and its conceptualization as a process wherein the internal contradictions of societies were ultimately resolved through change and upheaval, that Marx found particularly compelling. Later Marx would argue that at the heart of capitalism lay a fundamental contradiction between profit and wages: the pursuit of the former by the factory owner was inevitably pitted against the pursuit of wages by the factory worker. Marx argued that the motor of history derived from this contradiction and the struggle between social classes that it precipitated, predicting that a decisive battle would be fought once those classes had polarised into two rival blocks, the bourgeoisie and proletariat, with the latter destined to be triumphant.

A key concept in Marx's early writings was 'alienation', which he developed from his reading of Feuerbach, and which was central to both his criticisms of capitalism and of religions. For example, Marx argued that industrial technology transformed human labour into a series of repetitive, mechanical movements that rendered the worker 'both intellectually and physically to the level of a machine' (Marx 1992a: 285). In this way, the worker was alienated from work and from the products of work. But industrial technology also '*dehumanised*' workers (1992a: 336 italics in original) and therefore also alienated workers from what Marx called their 'species-being', a distinctive quality unique to human beings.

As for religions, Marx agreed with Feuerbach that 'the duplication of the world into a religious world and a secular one' caused 'self-alienation' (1992b: 422), but he went further, describing religions as 'the *opium* of the people' and that the 'call on them to give up ... illusions' was a '*call on them to give up a condition that requires illusions*' (1992c: 244; italics in original). Just as labour in the capitalist economy alienated the worker, so religions alienated the individual from the possibility of a better, more humane world in the here and now, rather than in some distant hereafter. But Feuerbach was not radical enough: it was one thing to expose God as a product of thought, it was another to see that thought as the product of a particular type of society in need of radical transformation. Hence at the end of the 'Theses on Feuerbach' Marx wrote that, 'The philosophers have only *interpreted* the world, in various ways; the point is to *change* it' (Marx 1992b: 423; italics in original).

The second observation concerns the claim, made by the French philosopher Louis Althusser, that Marx's thought underwent an intellectual shift around 1845, breaking from the vocabulary of German philosophy after which it was marked by his development of a new and distinctive

Introducing Marx

vocabulary, including 'base and superstructure', 'ideology', the 'relations of production', and the 'forces of production'. All of these concepts and terms can be found in the 'Preface' to *A Contribution to a Critique of Political Economy*, a piece of writing widely regarded as providing a clear summary of Marx's materialist approach to society, and which we will look at in more depth in the next chapter. This shift, according to Althusser, represented an intellectual break in Marx's thought, whereupon the Hegelian stamp of his early writings was left behind.

Let us conclude this introductory chapter with a summary of what we have covered so far:

- we have indicated the broad sweep of Marx's influence on the humanities, social sciences and theology, terrain that we will cover in more detail in the chapters that follow;
- we have noted the influence on Marx's thought of Hegel and Feuerbach, evident in Marx's approach to history and in concepts such as alienation;
- we have noted Althusser's suggestion that Marx's thought underwent a shift around 1845 from the early writings which are articulated in terms of philosophical, Hegelian ideas to the later writings which are more distinctive and sociological.

Question for discussion: Are religions 'the *opium* of the people'? Give reasons both for and against.

Chapter Two

Marx: Religion, Power, Ideology, and Change

Marx rarely wrote about religions directly. Rather, religions are discussed across a range of texts including 'A Contribution to a Critique of Hegel's Philosophy of Right', the 'Theses on Feuerbach', *The Communist Manifesto*, the 'Preface' to *A Contribution to a Critique of Political Economy* and volume I of *Capital*. The way Marx talks about religions shifts across these writings. In the early texts such as 'A Contribution to a Critique of

Marx: Religion, Power, Ideology, and Change

Hegel's Philosophy of Right' and the 'Theses on Feuerbach', Marx writes both with and against Feuerbach's account of alienation. Marx agrees with Feuerbach that religions are sources of self-alienation, but he goes beyond Feuerbach by suggesting that religions are social phenomena and, because they emerge from specific unequal arrangements of social relations, the critique of religions needs to be, at the same time, a critique of society. This is why, at the beginning of 'A Contribution to a Critique of Hegel's Philosophy of Right', Marx states that 'the criticism of religion is the prerequisite of all criticism' (Marx 1992c: 243). But Marx's references to religions are also made for literary and dramatic effect. For example, the opening lines of *The Communist Manifesto*, Marx and Engels make references to 'spectre[s]', 'exorcism[s]', and 'haunting', while in *Capital* in a section titled 'The Fetishism of Commodities', Marx turns to the metaphorical and rhetorical power of religions and religious concepts, notably 'fetishism'. For early sociologists such as Auguste Comte, the origins of religion lay in 'fetishism', which was characterised as the worship of things and objects. For Marx, the irrationality – as he saw it – of fetishism, anticipated the irrationality of capitalist society, as, according to Marx, in both objects valued more highly than people. However, our focus here is the 'Preface' to *A Contribution to a Critique of Political Economy*, which is widely regarded as providing the most succinct summary of Marx's materialist conception of society, his account of processes of social change and of ideology.

Isidore Auguste Marie François Xavier Comte (1798–1857) lived during the chaotic aftermath of the French Revolution. Like his contemporary Henri Saint-Simon (1760–1825), Comte wanted to bring an end to the uncertainties of his times by establishing a new, industrial society. It would be built on rational-secular principles and would be led by scientists, artists and industrialists. Comte argued that a new science was needed to carry out the task of reorganizing society. Initially he called the new science 'social physics' (Comte 1998: 159), but he later coined the term 'sociology' and, for this reason, he is regarded by many as sociology's founder, although Ibn Khaldun (1332–1406) offers an alternative genealogy for the discipline (see Soyer and Gilbert 2012). By the late 1830s, Comte had fleshed out a vision of the new science to include 'statics' and 'dynamics', the former to analyse the structure of a given society and the latter to consider its historical development. His sociology emerged not only from his analysis of the society of his day but also from his interest in the historical development of the sciences. Comte argued that the value of the sciences lay in their methods: he coined the term 'positivism' to distinguish scientific knowledge – which could be verified through the application of scientific methods such as observation and comparison – from religious knowledge, the earliest form of which was, or so he believed, fetishism. According to Comte, fetishism was the original stage of humanity, when people treated objects 'as if they were living beings' (Comte 1998: 147).

By the time he wrote the 'Preface', Marx had all but dispensed with the philosophical vocabulary he had inherited from Hegel and Feuerbach. The new language included 'base and superstructure', architectural metaphors which directed the reader to imagine that beneath the surface of society's everyday interactions and transactions there was a realm of deep structures and fundamental relationships that were ordinarily hidden from view. Take a moment to consider language. Every day you manipulate words and phrases to communicate in numerous social situations, some formal, some informal. You are a fluent speaker and yet, if you were asked to provide an outline of grammatical rules for a non-native speaker, you would very likely find the task if not impossible, then very difficult indeed. Now, just as one can be a fluent speaker of a language without necessarily being consciously aware of and able to explain its deep grammatical rules and structures, so one can be a competent member of society without really being able to say why society is the way it is. If we want to know about grammar and the structure of language, we can ask a linguist. Similarly, the purpose of marxist analysis – as with sociological analysis – is to bring to light the deep structures of society and to reveal them as the real causes of why society is the way it is.

As we have already noted, in the 'Preface' to *A Contribution to a Critique of Political Economy* Marx employed architectural metaphors. The base of society – 'the real foundation' – is where we find the relations of production, or what Marx called 'the economic structure of society' (1992d: 426). These are relationships which are central to society's ability to reproduce itself and endure through time. We are born into these relationships and they exist independently of us. But one of the most interesting aspects of Marx's model of society is that it is a dynamic model. The base is not static; the relations of production located there are neither fixed nor frozen. Marx claimed that when 'the material productive forces of society come into conflict with the existing relations of production . . . Then begins an era of social revolution. The changes in the economic foundation lead sooner or later to the transformation of the whole immense superstructure' (1992d: 425–6).

The nineteenth century when Marx was writing, was a period of intense technological change that witnessed the emergence of new technologies such as the steam engine and the beginnings of mass production in factories. Marx's point was that technological innovation was not neutral: as one technology replaced another, it caused changes in social and economic relations, which in turn led to changes in the wider organisation of society. Before the Industrial Revolution most people in England worked in agriculture and lived in the countryside, but by its end huge numbers had left to work in factories and to live in cities. Industrial society created a new social class of wealthy entrepreneurs and with them a range of new institutions and political and economic arrangements developed. Importantly, these changes were not painless and were accompanied by great suffering.

Marx also claimed that the base or structure of society actually shaped the way people think. In the gendered language of his time Marx stated that 'it is not the consciousness of men that determines their existence, but their social existence that determines their consciousness' (1992d: 425). Additionally, he claimed that not only consciousness and thought but also law, politics, religion, art, and philosophy were not independent realms of human activity but rather formed a 'superstructure', a vast collection of 'ideological forms in which men become conscious' (1992d: 426) of the changes taking place around them and through which they come to understand society. Critically, ideology was no neutral medium. The term had been coined in the eighteenth century by Antoine Louis Claude Destutt, Comte de Tracy (1754–1836) to denote a science of ideas, but it was deployed by Marx to explore how different forms of knowledge were implicated in the organisation of society and how they often reflected powerful interests. In *The German Ideology* Marx and Engels had argued that 'The ideas of the ruling class are in every epoch the ruling ideas' (Marx and Engels 1974: 64). In the 'Preface' Marx pointedly observed that 'just as one does not judge an individual by what he thinks about himself' so one cannot judge society by its religious, literary, or artistic expressions. Instead, those expressions 'must be explained from the contradictions of material life, from the conflict existing between the social forces of production and the relations of production' (1992d: 426).

Having distinguished the 'real foundation' or the economic base of society from the ideological 'superstructure' (1992d: 425) and having suggested that the former could be empirically specified 'with the precision of natural science' (1992d: 426), Marx was separating 'the real' from 'the ideological'. Marx was arguing that to understand society we need an objectivity that cannot be found in the subjective and partial (that is, ideological) perspective of religions or art. In *The German Ideology*, as in the 'Preface', Marx was searching for this objectivity – the 'critical attitude' (Marx and Engels 1974: 37) – just as a doctor seeks a diagnosis for a sick (or perhaps even a

Marx: Religion, Power, Ideology, and Change

deluded) patient. Marx seemed to be saying that his base-superstructure model of society offered a way through these problems of diagnosis, a way of overcoming ideology to ascertain why society is the way it is so that work could then begin to change it. But was not Marx part of, or inside, the very object (society) that he was studying? If so, on what basis could he claim to see society objectively, as if from the outside? And, if he could not, does that imply that all knowledge might be ideological, that is, might all knowledge be generated within and be saturated by the values and experiences of the time and place of its production?

A number of further questions follow from the way Marx talks about social change. For example, if we compare the way Marx talks about change in *The Communist Manifesto* and in the 'Preface', we can see that if *The Communist Manifesto* change occurs as a result of struggle between social classes – 'the history of all hitherto existing society is the history of class struggles' (1967: 79) – whereas in the 'Preface' change seems to be little more than a reflex response to technological innovation. Furthermore, if in *The Communist Manifesto* change occurs as a result of people developing their self-knowledge to change their circumstances, in the 'Preface' by contrast, change seems to occur independently of what people do, think, or say.

Finally, what about religions? According to Marx, religious change seems to be no more than a pale reflection of material change in the relations of production, at the base of society. But the theological disputes at the heart of the Reformation were arguably autonomous and separate from changes taking place elsewhere in sixteenth-century Europe, so perhaps Marx's model of base and superstructure is too simplistic and reductive. Even if we agree with Marx that we cannot entirely separate religious change such as that precipitated by Luther's attacks on the Catholic church from material, economic, and social relations and processes, we might argue that society is much more complex than Marx allows. For example, we might argue against Marx and in anticipation of Althusser and Gramsci that the superstructure is not simply a causal effect or pale reflection of the base, but instead argue that base and superstructure exist in a state of dynamic and interactive tension, with each exerting influence over the other.

Let us conclude this chapter with a quick summary of what we have covered so far:

- we have looked at some of the different ways in which Marx talked about religions in his writings;
- focusing on the 'Preface' to *A Contribution to a Critique of Political Economy*, we have looked at how religions are implicated in Marx's

base-superstructure model of society and social change;
- we have looked at the centrality of ideology to Marx's account of religions – we now have a good background in Marx which we can take forward as we explore marxist thought in more detail.

Question for discussion: Evaluate the utility of Marx's concept of ideology in relation to religions.

Chapter Three

Engels: The First Marxist Historian and Anthropologist of Religion

In this chapter we are going to look at Engels and his, by comparison with Marx, quite substantial writings on religions. We already know that Engels collaborated with Marx on important works such

Engels: The First Marxist Historian and Anthropologist

as *The German Ideology* and *The Communist Manifesto*. After Marx's death, Engels also played a significant role in shaping the reception of Marx, writing prefaces to various editions of *The Communist Manifesto* and *Capital* and editing and indeed altering the manuscripts to volumes II and III of *Capital* before publishing them. Given the close collaboration between the two of them across these texts, it is not always easy to see where Marx ends and Engels begins. Certainly, Engels was trying to secure the legacy of his friend. But he was also a writer and a thinker in his own right, conducting his own research and publishing under his own name. As such, we will look closely at three of Engels's books: *The Peasant War in Germany*, *Anti-Dühring*, and *Ludwig Feuerbach and the End of Classical German Philosophy*. In them, Engels draws not only from Marx but also from the sciences of his day and the widespread nineteenth-century enthusiasm for trying to create unified theories that combined scientific insights from disciplines such as biology, geology, and physiology with those of anthropology and sociology (see Stocking, Jr 1987). Our focus on these texts, rather than on his collaborations with Marx or on his voluminous correspondence with and about Marx, will allow us to engage with Engels and to recognise him as both the first marxist historian of religion and as the first marxist anthropologist of religion.

Religion and Marxism

Friedrich Engels was born in 1820 into a prosperous family in Barmen in what is today Germany and died in 1895 in London. Like Marx, he was strongly influenced by the writings of the Young Hegelians. In 1841 Engels was in Berlin for his national service, and while there he attended the university as a non-matriculated student, throwing himself enthusiastically into the debates and arguments of the day and in particular, Feuerbach's critique of Christianity. In 1842 Engels travelled to Manchester to work in his father's business. On his way he met Marx for the first time. But it was only later, in 1844 at a meeting in Paris, that their collaboration began. By this time Engels had already published numerous pamphlets and articles and he would continue to write prodigiously even as his partnership with Marx gathered pace. Unlike Marx, Engels had been raised in a deeply religious household and aged just nineteen had published his 'Letters from Wuppertal', a strident attack based on his own observations of social life, on the moral hypocrisy of the Protestant mill-owners of his home and their 'flexible conscience[s]' (Engels in Carver 2003: 3). Engels would re-employ these nascent ethnographic skills of observation and analysis in his ground-breaking account of working-class life in Manchester a few years later (Engels 1999). But it is to his later writings on religions that we must turn.

Engels: The First Marxist Historian and Anthropologist

The Peasant War in Germany has been described by Terrell Carver as setting the parameters of 'Marxian historiography' (Carver 2003: 41), while Engels himself has been described by David McLellan as 'the first Marxist to produce a sketch for a Marxist history of religion' (McLellan 1987: 36). Engels's basic argument was that the religious struggles of the Reformation in sixteenth century Germany were not simply theological disputes; behind them, an embryonic communist programme was emerging, and its principal protagonist was, according to Engels, Thomas Münzer (Boer 2011). According to Engels, Münzer's programme

> demanded the immediate establishment of the kingdom of God, the prophesied millennium, by restoring the Church to its original status and abolishing all the institutions that conflicted with this allegedly early-Christian, but, in fact, very much novel Church. By the kingdom of God Münzer understood a society without class differences, private property and a state authority independent of, and foreign to, the members of society. All the existing authorities, in so far as they refused to submit and join the revolution, were to be overthrown, all work and all property shared in common, and complete equality introduced. A union was to be established to realize all this, not only throughout Germany, but throughout all Christendom. (Engels 1967: 250–51)

Engels's fundamental claim was that Münzer's theology in fact articulated the political and economic interests of subordinate class groups. Norman Cohn's *The Pursuit of the Millennium: Revolutionary Millenarians and Mystical Anarchists in the Middle Ages* (1976), Eric Hobsbawm's *Primitive Rebels* (1959), and Peter Worsley's *The Trumpet Shall Sound* (1957) are classic examples of a twentieth-century Western marxist historiography of religions inspired directly by Engels's *The Peasant War in Germany*, and the compelling idea that religions do not simply legitimate the power of monarchs and states but, at times, can also be the vehicles for revolutionary sentiments and values. This double-sided view chimes of course with Marx's own ambivalent assessment of religions both as 'the sigh of the oppressed creature' and 'the heart of a heartless world' but also as the '*opium* of the people' able to delivery only '*illusory* happiness' (1992c: 244; italics in original).

However, elsewhere among Engels's writings, a slightly different approach to religions is laid out. In *Anti-Dühring*, a lengthy polemic attacking the works of Eugen von Dühring, Engels essentially adopts the 'intellectualist' and 'evolutionist' approach to religions taken by the British anthropologist E. B. Tylor (1832–1917):

> All religion, however, is nothing but the fantastic reflection in men's minds of those external

forces which control their daily life, a reflection in which the terrestrial forces assume the form of supernatural forces. In the beginnings of history it was the forces of nature which were first so reflected and which in the course of further evolution underwent the most manifold and varied personifications among the various peoples . . . But it is not long before, side by side with the forces of nature, social forces begin to be active – forces which confront man as equally alien and at first equally inexplicable, dominating him with the same apparent natural necessity as the forces of nature themselves. The fantastic figures, which at first only reflected the mysterious forces of nature, at this point acquire social attributes, become representatives of the forces of history. At a still further stage of evolution, all the natural and social attributes of the numerous gods are transferred to *one* almighty god. (Engels 1964a: 147–48)

It is important to point out that Engels was not writing here about the Reformation or the pious Protestantism of his upbringing, but was rather concerned with an imagined, original form of religion from which all the others had supposedly sprung. One of the great debates of late nineteenth and early twentieth-century anthropology and sociology concerned the origins of Religion (very much in the singular with a capital R). This involved trying to recapitulate the intellectual chain of reasoning which had led early humans to posit *super*natural and *meta*physical causes for natural, physical ones, and the postulation of a logical sequence of religious forms from the most 'primitive' (animism, fetishism, or totemism) to the most complex (monotheism). Of course, Engels's references to the 'forces of nature' and to 'social forces' cued him up to posit the natural sciences and marxism as signalling the demise of religions, insofar as they, with their basis in empirical observation, revealed the real forces at work behind nature and society. In *Ludwig Feuerbach and the End of Classical German Philosophy*, Engels articulated Tylor's theory of the origins of religion, namely that 'spirits are simply personified causes' (Tylor 1903 II: 108) and that monotheistic Christianity had evolved out of a much earlier religious form:

> From the very early times when men, still completely ignorant of the structure of their own bodies, under the stimulus of dream apparitions came to believe that their thinking and sensation were not activities of their bodies, but of a distinct soul which inhabits the body and leaves it at death – from this time men have been driven to reflect about the relation between this soul and the outside world. (Engels 1964b: 226)

Engels: The First Marxist Historian and Anthropologist

Sir Edward Burnett Tylor was born in 1832 to a prosperous Quaker family. He contracted tuberculosis in his early twenties and was advised to travel to a warmer climate. Tylor went to Mexico where he met the fellow Quaker and businessman Henry Christy (1810–1865). Tylor published an account of his travels in Mexico in 1861, and other books and articles followed, most significantly *Primitive Culture*, which was first published in two volumes in 1871. Tylor became the first professor of anthropology in 1896 at Oxford and died in 1917. Tylor's legacy in the anthropology of religion is complex: for example, Tylor claimed that the earliest form of religion was 'animism', which he defined as 'the belief in Spiritual Beings' (Tylor 1903 I: 424), but this is not taken seriously today. Yet, his insistence on the psychic unity of the species and his interest in human thought and universal, species-specific, cognitive processes that constrain and enable religious belief, is central to much contemporary research about religion. Perhaps the defining and today most discredited element of Tylor's anthropology was its evolutionism. Tylor imagined human history as a developmental process and by comparing the cultures and technologies of non-Western peoples to the industrial nation-states of Europe and America, Tylor concluded that the industrial-scientific nations of Europe and the West represented the pinnacle of human, social and intellectual evolution. This conclusion provided welcome legitimacy for Empire which assumed the benevolent and providential superiority of white, Western cultures and societies. Tylor's attempt to prove the origins of religion was bound up within these evolutionary assumptions (see Tremlett, Sutherland and Harvey 2017).

David McLellan has suggested that Engels's views were 'informed more by the rather undeveloped state of cultural anthropology at the time than by any recognisably Marxist orientation' (McLellan 1987: 36). However, it is clear that Marx also subscribed to the claims and arguments of intellectualists and evolutionists such as Tylor. For example, in the short section of the first volume of *Capital* called 'The Fetishism of Commodities', Marx used the idea of fetishism and the 'primitive delusions' of religion – specifically the assumption that things or fetishes were animate and alive and not simply inert matter – as a metaphor for capitalist society in which things and objects were sanctified and held in a higher regard than their human makers. In fact, both Marx and Engels were reading the anthropology of their time, but, with regard to religions, it was Engels who engaged most substantially with it so as to create the first marxist anthropology of religion.

Engels: The First Marxist Historian and Anthropologist

Like E. B. Tylor, Marx and Engels subscribed to a broadly evolutionary view of history as a developmental process characterised by, among other things, the waning significance of religion and the growing influence of science. This prediction of religious decline anticipated the secularization thesis which defined the post-WWII sociology of religion in Britain. According to Bryan Wilson (1982), quantitative data from the late nineteenth century – in particular church attendance figures – revealed the diminishing social significance of religious commitment in Britain. However, critics retorted that supporters of the thesis overestimated pre-modern levels of religious commitment. Critics also argued that declining participation in mainstream religions failed to account for growth in alternative spiritualities.

Let us conclude this chapter with a summary of what we have covered so far:

- we have noted the extent of the collaborative relationship between Engels and Marx;
- we have explored Engels's ambivalence about religions, both as sources of oppression and as vehicles for social protest and liberation;

- we have considered the influence of anthropology on Engels's and Marx's views on religions.

Question for discussion: 'Engels's approach to religions is in essence, a synthesis of Marx and Tylor'. Discuss, giving reasons both for and against the proposition.

Chapter Four

Hegemony, Ideology, and Religion: Althusser, Gramsci, and the Embrace of Uncertainty

In this chapter we are going to look at two twentieth-century thinkers who advanced new interpretations of Marx's work, developing new ideas and concepts in the process. We will begin with Louis Althusser who in the 1960s and

1970s was perhaps the most influential marxist philosopher in Europe. Althusser was born in Algeria in 1918. In 1937 he joined the Catholic group *Jeunesse étudiantes chrétiennes*, and his participation in Catholic organizations would continue even after he had joined the French Communist Party in 1948 (see Boer 2007). We already noted Althusser's claim in chapter I that Marx's thought underwent an intellectual shift around 1845, after which Marx dispensed with the intellectual concepts he had inherited from Hegel and Feuerbach and began developing his own and, according to Althusser, more distinctive, sociological vocabulary. Here we are going to focus on Althusser's essay 'Ideology and Ideological State Apparatuses (Notes Towards an Investigation)' (2008) in which he outlined a theory of ideology as a process through which individuals are called upon to perform particular roles in society.

Our second thinker is Antonio Gramsci. Gramsci was born in 1891 in Sardinia and was a founding member of the Italian Communist Party, which he led for a short time before being jailed in 1926 by Benito Mussolini, the fascist leader of Italy from 1922–1943. Gramsci would spend the rest of his life in jail – he died there in 1937 – but during his incarceration he would write his most important work, the *Prison Notebooks*. The *Notebooks* are notable because of Gramsci's interest in civil society and culture and the importance Gramsci gave to them as he sought to define Communist thought and strategy in the Italy of his day.

Althusser and Gramsci are important to us for two reasons: firstly because, for both of them, the Catholic Church is an important source of reflection, as an institution able to exercise enormous cultural power and influence and that is able to shape the manner in which individuals pursue their lives. Secondly, both Althusser and Gramsci re-configure the base-superstructure model that Marx developed in the preface to *A Contribution to a Critique of Political Economy*. Both Althusser and Gramsci suggest that superstructures and ideology enjoy autonomy from the economic base of society and, moreover, exert their own influence over it. For example, Althusser described 'the relative autonomy of the superstructure and the reciprocal action of the superstructure on the base' (Althusser 2008: 10). For Althusser and Gramsci, superstructures and ideology come to refer to culture in a broad sense, which in turn starts to be understood as a key site of struggle in processes of social reproduction rather than just as a passive reflection of the economic base. Importantly, the writings of Althusser and Gramsci have spurred further theoretical shifts including the post-marxism of Laclau and Mouffe (1985) and Hall's 'marxism without guarantees' (1986 and 2022).

Let us turn now to Althusser and his essay on ideology. In marxist theory the state has two aspects: first there is the repressive apparatus of the state such as the courts, the army, and the police. The repressive apparatus functions ultimately through violence. Then there is the ideological apparatus, which is made up of various bodies including religious institutions such as churches, educational institutions including schools and universities, the family, trades unions, sports clubs, cultural associations, and political parties. Althusser describes these ideological state apparatuses (ISAs) as 'multiple, distinct [and] relatively autonomous' (2008: 23) and he proposes a new theory of ideology as something which 'acts or functions in such a way that it recruits . . . or transforms individuals into subjects . . . by . . . *interpellation* or hailing [them]' (2008: 48). The ISAs, then, work not through violence but through transforming individuals into vehicles for carrying and spreading the values of the dominant culture.

Central to the essay is a comparison of the role of the church in feudal society and the role of schools in capitalist society. In the feudal period there was a small number of ISAs such as the family and the guilds, and one dominant one, which was the Catholic church. According to Althusser, participation in Catholic ritual practices such as Mass, prayer, or a funeral entailed the individual being called to perform in specific ways and to recognize her or himself and others as subjects of God and as virtuous and believing souls. These ritual practices demanded

Hegemony, Ideology and Religion

specific forms of bodily comportment, speech, and behaviour and ensured that the raw, biological material of human beings was channelled towards the creation of a subject that understood itself as having its own beliefs and ideas and saw its relationship with wider society as entirely natural when in fact it was a vehicle for the reproduction of society and society's dominant values.

In the feudal period the arena in which the struggle for social change took place was religion; the Reformation in the sixteenth century and then the French Revolution in the eighteenth saw the rise of the idea of the individual as a rational being, the limiting of the power of the church, and the eventual eclipse of the aristocracy and monarchy to be replaced by the secular state. The emergence of a new governing capitalist class and new institutions concerned with health, punishment, and education – hospitals, prisons, and schools – replaced some of the functions formerly carried out by the church. In modern capitalist societies, then, the dominant ISA is not the church but what Althusser calls the *'educational ideological apparatus'* (2008: 26; italics in original) and in particular, the school. According to Althusser, schools do not simply teach intellectual content such as sociology, but reinforce society's dominant norms and values, turning pupils and teachers like you and me into functioning members of society with roles, ambitions, talents, and expectations. But those roles, ambitions, talents, and expectations are not ours but are exactly what is required of us to secure the reproduction of capitalist society with its embedded and intersecting inequalities of class, race, and gender. 'Ideology', then, 'represents the imaginary relationship of individuals to their real conditions of existence' (2008: 36), by which Althusser means that we see our relationship to society in a way that both pleases us and deceives us.

Now many teachers and pupils are critical of society's dominant norms and values and are not simply passive vehicles for the reproduction of the ruling ideology. Indeed, it seems a quite obvious point that, in any given society, while we might agree that there are dominant values and ideas which we might call ideology, there are also spaces where people can and do think and live differently. Althusser's approach to ideology as an all-pervasive social cement that binds everything together seems to rule out the possibility of resistance from any quarter. The problem is, how to develop a model of society that is sufficiently dynamic as to be able to account both for the existence of elites, dominant classes, and hegemonic values, and for the existence of spaces, groups, and practices where alternative values are mobilised to contest the social consensus.

Hegemony, Ideology and Religion

Functionalism refers to the idea, in classical sociology, that societies are akin to bodies, and as such are made of up interlocking organs that work together to generate, in biological terms, homeostasis and in societal terms, stability. Early sociologists typically analysed religions in functionalist terms, that is as providers of shared values and ritual practices that enhanced the internal cohesion of social groups. However, the functionalist emphasis on solidarity has been criticised for its lack of dynamism and the difficulty of imagining social change. Althusser's approach to ideology has been criticised on the same grounds. Althusser claims that institutions such as the state, the Church and the family, function together to generate a kind of social cement that guarantees social reproduction, but as Stuart Hall has suggested, 'If the function of ideology is to reproduce capitalist social relations according to the requirements of the system, how does one account for subversive ideas or for ideological struggle?' (Hall 1986: 32).

Gramsci's interest in civil society was based in the realization that ideology was not a passive reflection of state power but an active force in its own right. For Gramsci, base and superstructure exist in a state of constant interaction and mutual influence, with neither assumed to be the primary causal nexus. He reached this conclusion having spent time reflecting on the revolutionary struggles of the early twentieth century in Russia, Germany, and Italy. Noting that only in Russia had the revolution succeeded, Gramsci concluded that in democratic societies where civil society included complex networks of trades unions, political associations including left-of-centre parties, as well as sports clubs, the media, schools, gardening clubs, and religious institutions among numerous others, revolution was virtually impossible.

Central to Gramsci's reflections on civil society was the Catholic church. Gramsci recognized that the church had played different roles in Italy's industrial north and in the agricultural south, sometimes acting as an ethical check on arbitrary power while at other times functioning to strengthen the hegemony of the dominant group or class. For Gramsci, the relationship of the church to the masses and the state during periods of both stability and upheaval provided a vital point of reflection for Communist political strategy. He understood that Communist strategy had to be long-term – what he called the 'war of position' – and that subaltern classes needed to establish alliances with a range of other social groups if they were going to be in a position to become the dominant force in society. As such he adopted the term 'hegemony' as a means of visualising society as a complex web of forces and alliances in which

Hegemony, Ideology and Religion

consent rather than domination was the key factor. For Gramsci, while the state has repressive functions, the dominant class was only able to sustain its dominance by aligning itself with 'the general interests of the subordinate groups' (1971: 182). As such, for Gramsci hegemony was 'a continuous process of formation and superseding of unstable equilibria ... in which the interests of the dominant group prevail, but only up to a certain point' (1971: 182), which means that hegemony could never be complete or total, and society was always therefore open to other ideas, practices, and possibilities.

Gramsci's conception of hegemony has been important to new developments in marxist thought, particularly in the writings of Chantal Mouffe and Ernesto Laclau, and of Stuart Hall, which have been critical of scientific marxism and which have drawn on theories, ideas, and concepts from outside the marxist tradition. For example, *In Hegemony and Socialist Strategy* (1985), Mouffe and Laclau draw on ideas of uncertainty and undecidability in how society is structured. That is, they complicate Marx's base-superstructure model of society and social change, rejecting its linearity and fixation with pre-determined causes and effects. Society is no longer defined in terms of a pre-determined historical trajectory towards freedom or constituted by specific social classes, one of which is destined to save and redeem the rest. Rather, Laclau and Mouffe foreground the social as a shifting field of struggles and possibilities. Stuart Hall argues along comparable lines, arguing against the sacrality of an ossified marxist tradition as a means of creating new spaces for radical thought and practice:

> But to have the sense that that world can only be understood by going to Marx as if his writings were indeed a sacred text, or a motto on the wall and all you need to do is embroider it a little and it will continue to come true, that marxism should be dead. (Hall 2022)

According to Hall, 'openness or relative indeterminancy is necessary to marxism itself as a theory' (1986: 43). For Hall, Marx does not offer a blueprint, and social change does not unfold according to the operation of fixed laws of development, but rather according to empirically specifiable moments of struggle and the contingent political strategies of the participants. Let us conclude with a summary:

- we have introduced Althusser's concept of ISAs;
- we have introduced Gramsci's conception of hegemony;
- we have reflected on how Althusser and Gramsci each modify Marx's conception of base-superstructure and of ideology;
- we have sketched some of the new developments in marxist thought inspired by the writings of Althusser and Gramsci.

Hegemony, Ideology and Religion

Question for discussion: 'Stuart Hall's embrace of uncertainty reveals the weakness of the conventional Marxist model of social change'. Discuss, developing arguments both for and against the proposal.

Chapter Five

The Frankfurt School: Horkheimer, Habermas, and Religion

The Institute for Social Research – which would later become known as the Frankfurt School – was founded in Germany in 1924. It was established with an endowment provided by the son of wealthy businessman Felix Weil, and the funds were sufficient to ensure that

The Frankfurt School

the institute, though formally attached to the University of Frankfurt, could operate more or less autonomously. When Max Horkheimer became the director of the institute in 1931 following the previous director Carl Grünberg's retirement, he brought together a diverse collection of scholars and thinkers with the intention of developing an interdisciplinary research programme in which sociologists, philosophers, economists, historians, and psychologists could work together to address the big questions of the day. But as the Nazi Party came to power in Germany the institute was forced moved first to Geneva in 1933, then to New York in 1935, and finally to California in 1941. These moves and the wider disruptions caused by the outbreak of WWII interrupted the work of the Institute, but by the early 1950s key members including Horkheimer had returned to what was by then West Germany, and the institute was re-established at the University of Frankfurt in 1953. These experiences, coupled with increasing disillusionment among members of the Frankfurt School with the direction of the Soviet Union, led to a wholesale re-evaluation of many of Marx's key ideas, focusing particularly on culture and ideology.

The writings of Max Weber (1864–1920), widely regarded as founder of the interpretive tradition of sociology, and Sigmund Freud (1856–1939), the founder of psychoanalysis, were extremely influential on the Frankfurt School, particularly for their focus on the body as a key site of struggle in capitalist societies. Weber's account of the Reformation as creating an 'iron cage' (Weber 2002: 123) of body-disciplined rationalism implicated in what he called 'the spirit of capitalism', and Freud's claim that civilization could only progress through the repression of embodied instincts and desires (Freud 1989), articulated a pessimistic account of modernity that contradicted Marx's conviction that the direction of history was towards increasing freedom (see Held 2004).

It was through the work of Herbert Marcuse (1898–1979) – who had joined the institute in 1933 – that the work of the Frankfurt School and its criticisms of mass culture and bureaucracy became well known, particularly among the Western, bohemian youth cultures of the 1960s. Marcuse's work combined insights from Sigmund Freud and Max Weber linking sexual repression with capitalist exploitation, which resonated with a counter–culture experimenting with new ideas

The Frankfurt School

and practices surrounding sex and embodied, transgressive experience, as well as practices and concepts drawn from Asian religions and cultures, from tantric yoga to Maoism. Today the Frankfurt School is best known for what Horkheimer called 'critical theory', and for the writings of the philosopher Jürgen Habermas. We will begin briefly with Horkheimer and his distinction between traditional and critical theory before moving on to sketch the fragmentary writings on religion composed towards the end of his life. We will then turn to Habermas and his distinction between the system and the lifeworld and his notion of communicative action, before examining his later engagements with religion.

Max Horkheimer was born in 1895 near Stuttgart into a wealthy Jewish family. He left school to become an apprentice in his father's textile factory, but after being introduced to philosophy and sociology he went to the University of Frankfurt. On becoming director of the institute, he published a number of essays including 'Critical and Traditional Theory', published in 1937, which is notable for his insistence that the conventional idea of social science as the disinterested pursuit of truth obscured the extent to which facts were not simply lying around waiting to be picked up and analysed by social scientists but were established through the process of social scientific analysis itself. As such, Horkheimer argued that facts were not neutral but were saturated by the values of the scientist and of wider society. According to Horkheimer, traditional theory only appeared objective; in reality, it did little more than affirm the existing structures of society. The whole point of critical theory was to conduct research in a manner guided explicitly by values of freedom and as such contribute to the progressive transformation of society. As director of the institute he therefore set about creating an ambitious programme of interdisciplinary research. However, alongside other members of the Frankfurt School, Horkheimer was severely shaken by the Nazification of Germany and Stalin's reign of terror in the Soviet Union. Increasingly disenchanted by the enthusiastic participation of the masses in nationalism and consumerism and by the tendency on the left for political dogmatism, Horkheimer turned to religion which, he suggested, sustained an impulse for change towards a better world. In an interview in 1970 Horkheimer claimed that in the pursuit of a more just society 'the role of faith' was central, stating that religion and theology implied an 'awareness that the world is appearance, that it is not the absolute truth, the last [word]' (Horkheimer in Brittain 2005: 163). These remarks did not go down well with some commentators, who accused him of abandoning materialism.

Jürgen Habermas was born in 1929. From 1956 he studied under Horkheimer at the Institute for Social Research and was active in the German

The Frankfurt School

anti-nuclear movement in the 1950s and in the student protests of the 1960s. He was also critical of those German intellectuals who had been complicit with the Nazi regime, such as the philosopher Martin Heidegger (1889–1976). In 1964 Habermas was appointed Horkheimer's successor at the Institute, where he continued Horkheimer's critique of traditional theory.

Donna Haraway (b. 1944) was born in Denver in the USA. She studied philosophy and theology in Paris on a Fulbright Scholarship and completed a PhD in biology at Yale. Haraway's work explores borderlands between theology, science, and feminism, asserting the embodied and situated nature of knowledge against the gendered 'god trick of seeing everything from nowhere' (Haraway 1991a: 189). Haraway's interest in science and technology challenges normative divisions between organism and machine. Her provocation 'I'd rather be a cyborg than a goddess' (1991b: 181) poses the possibility of a 'socialist-feminism' (1991b: 149) constructed out of the image of the cyborg, a transgressive entity that is neither human nor machine. Her writing works with and against the grain of the Frankfurt School and its critique of Enlightenment conceptions of rationality, value-free neutrality, and objectivity.

Religion and Marxism

In his major work, *The Theory of Communicative Action*, Habermas set out to diagnose the structural and systemic problems of modern societies, which he framed in terms of a contradiction between the 'system' on the one hand, and the 'lifeworld' – which included religions – on the other. Drawing in interdisciplinary fashion from linguistics, philosophy, and sociology, Habermas argued that the bureaucratic-administrative and economic systems were characterised by a means-end, purposive rationality that prioritised forms of action based in egoistic calculations of utility and success. For Habermas, these systems and their operating rationality were the outcome of the Enlightenment and wider processes of secularization and disenchantment inherent in capitalism. By contrast, the lifeworld was a realm of implicit shared values, norms, and symbolic meanings responsible for cultural reproduction, social integration and socialization that included cultural and religious forms and practices. According to Habermas, the lifeworld is 'always present', it is 'intuitively familiar' a 'reservoir of taken-for-granteds' (Habermas 1987: 110), and a '*preinterpreted* domain' (1987: 114) and is constituted through dialogue. Habermas claims that the lifeworld is shaped by what he calls 'communicative action', a form of action where individuals orient themselves towards others not according to egoistic criteria of utility or success

The Frankfurt School

but rather in terms of reaching consensus and agreement with one another.

In modern societies, according to Habermas, the lifeworld is threatened with colonisation by the forms of administrative and economic rationality characteristic of the bureaucratic and economic systems, an outcome which would have serious negative ramifications for the stability of wider society. Habermas's solution is to explore what he calls 'communicative rationality' – the rationality of the lifeworld as a counter to the means-end, ego-oriented rationality of capitalism. According to Habermas, implicit in every speech-act or utterance is an orientation towards another person and towards agreement. Communicative action orients us to understand others, and Habermas's objective is to 'preserve the lifeworld and bring out its fundamental core, which is to serve the normative self-regulation of society' (Furseth and Repstad 2006: 51) and thereby provide a new basis for modernity.

At the centre of Habermas's work and of his engagement with religions is communication and reason as they are materialized through dialogue in specific institutional, social, and domestic spaces and contexts. In a series of essays gathered together under the title *Between Naturalism and Religion* published in English in 2008, Habermas discusses the emergence of a global public sphere. Noting the increasingly objectifying gaze of the hard sciences justified on the basis of rapid, ongoing technological innovation on the one hand and the continuing vitality of religions and the spread of forms of religious fundamentalism on the other, Habermas explores the sites and occasions in which religious and secular citizens can recognise one another and engage in dialogue. According to Habermas, such dialogues can only occur once all sides are willing to acknowledge the limits of their respective perspectives. Critical of both religious and secular-rationalist or scientific forms of fundamentalism, Mendieta argues that Habermas is concerned with 'rescuing for the modern liberal state those motivational and moral resources that it cannot generate or provide itself' (Mendieta 2011: 236), which points to the importance, for Habermas, of communicative action as a cognitive and social resource that can reaffirm modernity and the vision of a pluralist, democratic society.

Let us conclude this chapter with a brief summary of what we have covered:

- we have introduced the Frankfurt School;
- we have introduced Horkheimer's concept of critical theory;
- we have noted the interdisciplinary approaches of Horkheimer and Habermas, which have placed Marx's thought in dialogue with other disciplines including philosophy, psychology, sociology and linguistics;

The Frankfurt School

- we have introduced Habermas's concept of communicative action and explored the extent to which his interest in religions is related to his wider project of developing cognitive and socio-ethical resources to support democratic society.

Question for discussion: 'The sociology of religions should not seek neutrality or value-free detachment'. Discuss, providing arguments both for and against the proposal.

Chapter Six

Marxism and Liberation Theology

Liberation theology is a term that was originally applied to a particular kind of contextual theology that emerged in Latin America in the 1960s, which prioritised critical reflection on lived experience rather than the study of abstract ideas in the seminary. Some have argued that liberation theology was anticipated in sixteenth-century debates about the ethics of evangelization

Marxism and Liberation Theology

in the New World and nineteenth-century Latin American anti-colonial struggles. Certainly, during the 1960s, Latin America was struggling with widespread poverty and dictatorship, and it was recognized in some circles that there was a need to change the dominant economic and political structures of Latin American societies. Priests began to involve themselves in local struggles against injustice, and a new, politically engaged theological practice emerged that was largely external to the church's institutional structures and which, moreover, drew implicitly from marxist ideas for social transformation.
It also drew from the meetings of Vatican II which, according to the Filipino Bishop Labayen in his book *Revolution and the Church of the Poor* (1995), created spaces for the church to critically reflect on its mission. 'Out of this self-scrutiny', wrote Labayen, 'came the resolve for the Catholic Church to become the *Church of the Poor*', allowing it to leave behind 'the centuries-old Christendom model with its face of neo-cultural imperialism and neo-colonialism' (Labayen 1995: 37). As this quote from a Filipino bishop indicates, liberation theology may have originated in Latin America, but it soon spread to Asia and indeed to Africa, that is to countries with comparable experiences of poverty and dictatorship. And in the Philippines as in Latin America and Africa a crucial dimension of this

53

new theology was the dialogue that emerged between the church and the left. That this new theology refused political neutrality in the face of injustice, that it was focused on the experience of the poor, and finally that it was conceived as a praxis – that is as a combination of social engagement and theological reflection – put it at odds with traditional theology, which had so often served the interests of the status quo. For liberation theologians, the church was to be a force for progressive social change. The point of departure, then, for liberation theology was 'not detached reflection on Scripture and tradition' but 'the shanty towns and land struggles, the lack of basic amenities, the carelessness about the welfare of human persons, the death squads and the shattered lives of refugees' (Rowland 2007: 2).

Marxism and Liberation Theology

Central to marxism is power. The sociologist Max Weber understood power in terms of the capacity of a social actor to exert power over another. Weber's emphasis on actor agency can be contrasted with broadly functionalist and marxist approaches which locate power in social structures and systems rather than in individuals. However, whereas functionalist theories stress the integrative dynamics of social systems, marxist theories emphasise inequality and conflict. In *Discipline and Punish* (1991), The influential French philosopher Michel Foucault explored what he called the 'microphysics' of power to argue that in modern societies with their prisons, schools and factories, power was not so much exercised to repress or to dominate individuals but actually generated new systems of knowledge through which to classify, punish, train and monitor them. Foucault's approach to power in terms of knowledge was taken up by a number of post-colonial intellectuals including Edward Said in *Orientalism* (1979).

Today, Latin American, African, and Asian countries including the Philippines remain gripped by injustice and inequality and the Catholic church has lost influence across these regions as new, charismatic, Pentecostal and evangelical churches have emerged armed with the so-called 'prosperity gospel' that has energised populations previously receptive to the theology of liberation. A key question to ask, then, is whether liberation theology failed? To be sure, certain quarters in the Catholic church regarded any kind of dialogue with marxism with suspicion. In 1984 the Vatican published an *Instruction on Certain Aspects of the Theology of Liberation*, which warned of the dangers of divergence that might arise from the careless use of concepts borrowed from marxist thought (see Turner 2007: 229). Given that, from a certain theological point of view, marxism was intrinsically 'reductivist' and 'connected with a praxis of class hatred and struggle . . . and the denial of God' (2007: 231), significant voices in the Church were not sympathetic to interdisciplinary collaboration with what they regarded as a 'general theory of society and history . . . ideologically committed to atheism, materialism and reductivism' (2007: 233). By contrast, others argued that liberation theology had failed because it simply wasn't marxist enough (Turner 2007:233). However, a more thoughtful position is that it didn't fail but was merely one step in a longer process; it is worth reflecting on the fact that the creative synthesis of Catholic theology with marxism has created new spaces for women, black, queer, and indigenous peoples to be able to articulate new, more inclusive theologies and, more recently, for the articulation of new eco-theologies. In what follows, we will examine some of the ideas of some of the figures in the

Marxism and Liberation Theology

liberation theology tradition, including the 'father' of liberation theology Gustavo Gutierrez as well as Paolo Freire and Otto Maduro, and the less well-known Ivone Gebara.

Gustavo Gutierrez was born in 1928 and is widely regarded as the founder of liberation theology (Goizueta 2019). Gutierrez had initially studied to become a psychiatrist. However, after three years he changed direction, entering the seminary before studying psychology in Belgium and then theology in France before being ordained in 1959. According to Gutierrez, theology in the Global North – that is in Europe and North America – had, since the advent of the modern era in the nineteenth century, developed in response to the unbelieving atheist. By contrast, for theologians in Latin America, the challenge came not from non-believers but from non-persons, 'those who are not recognized as people by the existing social order: the poor, the exploited, those systematically and legally deprived of their status as human beings', In this context theology came down to the question of 'how to proclaim God as Father in a world that is inhumane' (Gutierrez 2007: 28). As such, Gutierrez's theology rests on two ideas: firstly, that theology must be grounded in the lived experience of the people and secondly, that it cannot remain aloof or neutral in the face of the suffering of the people.

Another major contributor to liberation theology was Paolo Freire, who was born in 1921 in Brazil. In 1963 he was made responsible for a national literacy campaign, but following a military coup the following year, Freire was jailed and then exiled. While in prison he wrote *Pedagogy of the Oppressed*, in which he developed an idea for education not simply as the transfer of technical skills and dominant values but as the awakening, on the part of the learner, of personal and social awareness and what he described as 'rebellious doubt' and 'a curiosity not easily satisfied'. Freire worked with the World Council of Churches in Geneva before being allowed to return to Brazil in 1979. Freire was not a priest but a married layman, yet his writings are seen as having made a substantial contribution to liberation theology for his stress on education as a kind of praxis. He died in 1997 in Brazil.

Otto Maduro was born in 1945 in Venezuela. He pursued postgraduate studies in the sociology of religion in Belgium, before embarking on an academic career as a theologian. He described himself as an *agent provocateur* and his role as a teacher as 'not so much transmitting knowledge as eliciting doubts, questions, and quests' among his students (Kearns, Spickard and Ortega-Aponte 2014: 25). In his introduction to the English language edition of *Maps for a Fiesta*, published shortly after he passed away in 2013, Eduardo Mendieta reflected on Maduro's life, stating that he had been 'preoccupied with how suffering, subaltern, marginalized and disempowered subjects produce knowledge' (2015: xiii). Like Gutierrez and Freire, Maduro's approach to knowledge and learning was as *praxis*, a transformative activity very different from education simply as training to work, and which was based in an explicit dialogue between theology and marxism but also sociology. Above all, Maduro's interest was in asking questions in support of 'open-mindedness, pluralism, curiosity, research, critical reflection, discussion, and creative imagination' and as a means of challenging 'unreflective certainties, close-mindedness, dogmatism, [and] fear' (Maduro 2015: 103), so that the 'cry of the oppressed' (Maduro 2015: 166) is heard.

> The dominant paradigm in the sociology of religion today is 'lived religion'. Lived religion attends to 'how religion and spirituality are practiced, experienced and expressed by ordinary people (rather than official spokespersons) in the context of their everyday lives' (McGuire 2008: 12). Advocates of the secularization thesis typically gather and evaluate quantitative data to determine macro-level shifts in religious behaviour and identification. By contrast, lived religion works with qualitative data to enable the 'thick description' of religious lives. The approach typically privileges individuals and communities not as bearers of orthodoxy or carriers of theologically correct beliefs, but as creative makers of meaning.

Ivone Gebara was born in 1944 in Brazil, the child of Middle Eastern immigrants. She studied philosophy and entered the Augustinian Order of the Sisters of our Lady in 1967. She later travelled to Belgium to study philosophy and theology before taking a post at the Theological Institute of Recife, where she also conducted pastoral work and wrote her doctoral thesis on the French philosopher Paul Ricoeur. Gebara's writings have explored issues from patriarchy and feminism to the links between the exploitation of the poor and of nature. In 1995 she was forbidden from expressing herself in speech or writing by the Vatican, following remarks published in the Brazilian magazine *Veja* that 'abortion is not a sin' (Fernandes 2022: 98). According to Silvia Fernandes, Gebara's 'efforts to bring liberation theology into conversation with feminism and ecological thinking have been truly pioneering' while her call for greater flexibility in relation to issues such as 'sexuality, the body, and the role of women in the Church' positions her at the 'leading edge of a Catholicism in productive flux and a Christianity built by a growing number of diverse and articulate voices from the Global South' (2022: 99).

Let us conclude this chapter with a brief summary of what we have covered:

- we have outlined the emergence of liberation theology;
- we have introduced some of the key voices in liberation theology;

Marxism and Liberation Theology

- we have noted some of the principal features of liberation theology including its emphasis on lived experience over the study of Scripture and for the space it has made for women, black, queer and indigenous peoples to articulate new, more inclusive theologies and, more recently, for the articulation of new eco-theologies.

Question for discussion: Critically evaluate the claim that marxism is incompatible with theology. Your response should include reasons both for and against.

Chapter Seven

Conclusions

An introductory book such as this cannot offer a complete picture and is never the final word. Neither marxism nor religions are complete objects – they are constantly changing fields of thought, practice, and interpretation. Moreover, the relationship between them – here antagonistic, there in dialogue – is unfixed and indeterminate. As such, a book about marxism and religions can only ever be a provisional document. Nevertheless, I hope that this book has given you a sense of the different ways in which marxists talk about

Conclusions

religions and about how those conversations intersect with wider debates in the humanities and social sciences, and in the sociology of religions.

I want to conclude with three points: firstly, we have seen that Marx's thought emerged at a turbulent moment in European history. Serial revolutions in technology, ideas, and politics, combined with a growing awareness of other societies and cultures with their own histories, voices, and experiences, had brought Europe to a crisis point. Marx developed his ideas as a means of explaining this crisis. Marx wanted to help us understand the opaque and mysterious forces of rapid and disorienting social change, insisting that however monstrous or demonic they at first appeared, they could in fact be named, tamed, and brought under common control. For Marx, religions – particularly the 'primitive' religions of the nineteenth century anthropological imagination – provided metaphorical resources for the critique of capitalism. More fundamentally, Feuerbach's critique of Christianity had bequeathed to both Marx and Engels a set of arguments and concepts that mobilised their dual account of religions, on the one hand as powerful institutions that legitimated the social order and on the other as potent vehicles of social protest. Moreover, Marx's claim that 'the criticism of religion is the prerequisite of all criticism' (Marx 1992c: 243), set up the study of religions as a fundamental barometer of the social and the critique of power.

Secondly, we have seen that Marx's account simplified historical processes of change, their direction, and their causes and their effects, and later thinkers modified Marx's ideas while retaining the central aim of developing a theory of society committed to improving the life experiences of all. Althusser, Gramsci, the Frankfurt School, and the theologians of liberation all remained committed to a recognizably marxist research agenda committed to advancing social justice while, at the same time, bringing marxism into new, interdisciplinary conversations and enriching it in the process.

Thirdly and finally, we have seen that religions – and particularly the Catholic church – have provided an important source of reflection for many of our marxist thinkers. That the Catholic Church features so heavily here is of course partly because the majority of our focus has been on European thinkers, and partly also because, when our focus has been on the global south, we have been considering contexts heavily shaped by the hubris and violence of colonialism and evangelizing missions.

Glossary

Alienation: term derived from the writings of Hegel and Feuerbach. It refers to processes through which human beings are estranged from themselves, for example through dehumanizing labour and/or through the splitting of the world into religious and secular domains.

Base: the first of two architectural metaphors for society developed by Marx, it refers to the economic foundation of social life. See also *Superstructure*.

Critical Theory: associated with the Frankfurt School, critical theory refers to a research programme developed not in the interests of securing dispassionate neutrality and objectivity, but which is guided by values and ideals of social justice.

Forces of Production: refers to the technologies operating at the economic base of society. Technological innovation is a major driver of social change due to the shifts it generates in the relations of production. See *Mode of Production* and *Relations of Production*.

Hegemony: a term associated with the writings of Gramsci, hegemony refers to the alliances and relationships through which a dominant group establishes consensus in democratic societies. See *Ideology*.

Ideology: a term used by Marx to investigate the relationships between specific ideas and particular forms of society, and the extent to which ideas may prevent critical analysis of society. See *Superstructure*.

Interdisciplinary: The humanities and the social and natural sciences are divided into disciplines (history, sociology, biology, etc) with their own domains of enquiry and their own theories and methods for asking questions and pursuing research. 'Interdisciplinary' means combining elements from different disciplines to generate new theories and new methods as well as new directions for research.

Glossary

Interpellation: a term used by Althusser to describe the process through which individuals internalise social norms and develop identities.

Lifeworld: associated with the work of Habermas, the lifeworld refers to a constellation of shared values and social practices of everyday life, distinct from the egoism and rationalism of the economic and bureaucratic spheres.

Mode of Production: every society must reproduce itself through time. Mode of production can refer narrowly just to the specific combination of the relations of production and the forces of production in a society, but it can also refer more widely to the ensemble of institutions and social practices through which reproduction is secured. See *Forces of Production* and *Relations of Production*.

Praxis: creative and self-transforming activity.

Reductionism: a type of analysis in which complex phenomena are explained through recourse to a single cause or basic principle.

Relations of Production: refers to the relations between workers and owners in capitalist society or between peasants and lords in feudal society. It points to the importance of analysing the structured relations between different social groups in society. See *Forces of Production* and *Mode of Production*.

Superstructure: the second of two architectural metaphors for society developed by Marx, it refers to the realm of ideas and draws attention to the relationship between ideas and society. See *Base* and *Ideology*.

References

Althusser, Louis. 2008. 'Ideology and State Apparatuses (Notes towards an Investigation)'. In *On Ideology*, Louis Althusser, 1–60. London: Verso.

Berenson, Edward. 1984. *Populist Religion and Left-Wing Politics in France, 1830–1852*. Princeton, NJ: Princeton University Press, 1984.

Bhambra, Gurminder, K. 2011. 'Talking among Themselves? Weberian and Marxist Historical Sociologies as Dialogues without Others'. *Millennium: Journal of International Studies* 39: 667–81. https://doi.org/10.1177/0305829811401119.

Boer, Roland. 2007. 'Althusser's Catholic Marxism'. *Rethinking Marxism* 19, no. 4: 469–86. https://doi.org/10.1080/08935690701571128.

Boer, Roland. 2011. 'Opium, Idols and Revolution: Marx and Engels on Religion'. *Religion Compass* 5, no. 11: 698–707. https://doi.org/10.1111/j.1749-8171.2011.00317.x.

Brittain, Christopher Craig. 2005. 'Social Theory and the Premise of All Criticism: Max Horkheimer on Religion'. *Critical Sociology* 31, nos. 1–2: 153–68. https://doi.org/10.1163/1569163053084379.

Carver, Terrell. 2003. *Engels: A Very Short Introduction*. Oxford: Oxford University Press, 2003.

Cohn, Norman. 1976. *The Pursuit of the Millennium: Revolutionary Millenarians and Mystical Anarchists in the Middle Ages*. New York: Oxford University Press.

Comte, Auguste. 1998. 'Philosophical Considerations on the Sciences and the Scientists'. In *Comte: Early Political Writings*, edited by H. S. Jones, 145–86. Cambridge: Cambridge University Press.

Engels, Friedrich. 1964a. 'Anti-Dühring'. In *Karl Marx and Friedrich Engels on Religion*, 145–51. New York: Schocken Books.

Engels, Friedrich. 1964b. 'Ludwig Feuerbach and the End of Classical German Philosophy'. In *Karl Marx and Friedrich Engels on Religion*, 213–68. New York: Schocken Books.

Engels, Friedrich. 1967. *Engels: Selected Writings*. London: Penguin.

Engels, Friedrich. 1999. *The Condition of the Working Class in England*. Oxford: Oxford University Press, 1999.

Fernandes, Silvia. 2022. *Christianity in Brazil: An Introduction from a Global Perspective*. London: Bloomsbury.

Foucault, Michel. 1991. *Discipline and Punish: The Birth of the Prison*. Harmondsworth: Penguin.

Freud, Sigmund. 1989. *Civilization and Its Discontents*. New York: W. W. Norton.

Furseth, Inger, and Pål Repstad. 2006. *An Introduction to the Sociology of Religion: Classical and Contemporary Perspectives*. London: Routledge.

Goizueta, Roberto, S. 2019. 'Liberation Theology I: Gustavo Gutierrez'. In *The Wiley Blackwell Companion to Political Theology*, edited by William T. Cavanaugh and Peter Manley Scott, 280–92. Chichester: John Wiley & Sons.

References

Gramsci, Antonio. 1971. 'The Modern Prince'. In *Selections from the Prison Notebooks of Antonio Gramsci*, edited and translated by Quintin Hoare and Geoffrey Nowell Smith, 125–205. London: Lawrence & Wishart.

Gutierrez, Gustavo. 2007. 'The Task and Content of Liberation Theology'. In *The Cambridge Companion to Liberation Theology*, edited by Christopher Rowland, 19–38. Cambridge: Cambridge University Press.

Habermas, Jürgen. 1987. *The Theory of Communicative Action Volume II: Lifeworld and System: A Critique of Functionalist Reason*, translated by Thomas McCarthy. Cambridge: Polity Press.

Habermas, Jürgen. 2008. *Between Naturalism and Religion: Philosophical Essays*. Cambridge: Polity Press.

Hall, Stuart. 1983. 'For a Marxism without Guarantees'. *Australian Left Review* 84, no.1 (1983): 38–43.

Hall, Stuart. 1986, 'The Problem of Ideology – Marxism without Guarantees'. *Journal of Communication Inquiry* 10, no. 2: 28–44. https://doi.org/10.1177/019685998601000203.

Haraway, Donna. 1991a. 'Situated Knowledges: The Science Question in Feminism in the Late Twentieth Century'. In *Simians, Cyborgs and Women: The Reinvention of Nature*, Donna Haraway, 183–201. London: Free Association Books.

Haraway, Donna. 1991b. 'A Cyborg Manifesto'. In *Simians, Cyborgs and Women: The Reinvention of Nature*, Donna Haraway, 149–81. London: Free Association Books.

Hegel, Georg. 1941. W. F. *Lectures on the Philosophy of History*, translated by John Sibree. London: G. Bell and Sons.

Held, David. 2004. *Introduction to Critical Theory: Horkheimer to Habermas*. Cambridge: Polity Press.

Hobsbawm, Eric. 1959. *Primitive Rebels: Studies in Archaic Forms of Social Movement in the 19th and 20th Centuries*, Manchester: Manchester University Press.

Kearns, Laurel, James Spickard, and Elias Ortega-Aponte. 2014. 'In Memoriam: Otto Maduro'. *Journal of the American Academy of Religion* 82, no. 1: 22–29. https://doi.org/10.1093/jaarel/lft111.

Labayen, Julio, Xavier. 1995. *Revolution and the Church of the Poor*. Manila: Socio-Pastoral Institute and Clareton Publications.

Laclau, Ernesto, and Chantal Mouffe. 1985. *Hegemony and Socialist Strategy*. London: Verso.

Maduro, Otto. 2015. *Maps for a Fiesta: A Latina/o Perspective on Knowledge and the Global Crisis*. New York: Fordham University Press.

Marx, Karl. 1992a. 'Economic and Philosophical Manuscripts'. In *Karl Marx: Early Writings*, translated by Rodney Livingstone and Gregor Benton, 279–400. London: Penguin.

Marx, Karl. 1992b. 'Theses on Feuerbach'. *Karl Marx: Early Writings*, translated by Rodney Livingstone and Gregor Benton, 421–23. London: Penguin.

Marx, Karl. 1992c. 'A Contribution to the Critique of Hegel's Philosophy of Right: Introduction'. In *Karl Marx: Early Writings*, translated by Rodney Livingstone and Gregor Benton, 243–57. London: Penguin.

Marx, Karl. 1992d. 'Preface to a Contribution to a Critique of Political Economy'. In *Karl Marx: Early Writings*, translated by Rodney Livingstone and Gregor Benton, 424–28. London: Penguin.

Marx, Karl, and Friedrich Engels. 1967. *The Communist Manifesto*. London: Penguin.

Marx, Karl, and Friedrich Engels. 1974. *The German Ideology*, edited by C. J. Arthur. London: Lawrence and Wishart.

McGuire, Meredith B. 2008. *Lived Religion: Faith and Practice in Everyday Life*. Oxford: Oxford University Press.

McLellan, David. 1987. *Marxism and Religion: A Description and Assessment of the Marxist Critique of Christianity*. New York: Harper & Row.

References

Mendieta, Eduardo. 2011. 'Rationalization, Modernity and Secularization'. In *Jürgen Habermas: Key Concepts*, edited by Barbara Fuller, 222–38. Durham: Acumen.

Mendieta, Eduardo. 2015. 'Introduction'. In *Maps for a Fiesta: A Latino Perspective on Knowledge and the Global Crisis*, Otto Maduro, edited by Eduardo Mendieta, vii–xiii. New York: Fordham University Press.

Pilbeam, Pamela. 2000. 'Dream Worlds? Religion and the Early Socialists in France'. *The Historical Journal* 43, no. 2: 499–515. https://doi.org/10.1017/S0018246X99008924.

Rowland, Christopher. 2007. 'Introduction: The Theology of Liberation'. In *The Cambridge Companion to Liberation Theology*, edited by Christopher Rowland, 1–16. Cambridge: Cambridge University Press.

Said, Edward, W. 1979. *Orientalism*. New York: Vintage Books.

Soyer, Mehmet, and Paul Gilbert. 2012. 'Debating the Origins of Sociology: Ibn Khaldun as a Founding Father of Sociology'. *International Journal of Sociological Research* 5, nos. 1–2: 13–30.

Stocking, George W., Jr. 1987. *Victorian Anthropology*. New York: The Free Press.

Tremlett, Paul-François, Liam T. Sutherland, and Graham Harvey. 2017. 'Introduction: Why Tylor, Why Now?' In *Edward Burnett Tylor, Religion and Culture*, edited by Paul-François Tremlett, Liam T. Sutherland, and Graham Harvey, 1–7. London: Bloomsbury.

Turner, Denys. 2007. 'Marxism and Liberation Theology'. In *The Cambridge Companion to Liberation Theology*, edited by Christopher Rowland, 229–47. Cambridge: Cambridge University Press.

Tylor, Edward, B. 1903. *Primitive Culture: Researches into the Development of Mythology, Philosophy, Religion, Language, Art and Custom Vols. I & II*, 4th ed. London: John Murray.

Weber, Max. 2002. *The Protestant Ethic and the Spirit of Capitalism*. London: Routledge.

Religion and Marxism

Wilson, Bryan. R. 1982. *Religion in Sociological Perspective*. Oxford: Oxford University Press.

Worsley, Peter. 1957. *The Trumpet Shall Sound: A Study of 'Cargo' Cults in Melanesia*. London: Macgibbon and Kee.

About the Author

Paul-François Tremlett is a senior lecturer in religious studies at the Open University. His research interests include classical and contemporary anthropological and sociological theories of religion and the broad constitution of religion as a site of study in societies experiencing rapid social change. He is the author of *Towards a New Theory of Religion and Social Change: Sovereignties and Disruptions* (Bloomsbury 2021) and co-edited *Ritual and Democracy: Protests, Publics and Performances* (Equinox, 2020). He also co-edits the Bloomsbury Series 'Religion, Space and Place'.

Index

abortion 60
action, communicative 45, 48–51
Africa 6, 53, 55
Algeria 32
alienation 7–8, 9, 11, 65
  self- 8
Althusser, Louis vii, 8–9, 18, 31–7, 40, 64, 67
America, United States of 27, 57
animism 26–7

anti-nuclear movement 47
anomie 2
anthropology 1, 24–5, 30, 63
  of religion 21, 27–8
anti-Semitism 3
architectural metaphors 13–14, 65, 68
atheism 56, 57

Barmen, Germany 22
Belgium 4, 57, 58, 60

Index

Berlin, Germany 3, 22
biology 21, 35, 37, 47, 66
Blanc, Louis x
Bonn, Germany 3
bourgeois epoch 2
bourgeoisie 7
Brazil. 57–8, 60
Buchez, Philippe-Joseph-Benjamin x–xi
Buddhism ix

Cabet, Étienne x–xi
California, USA 43
'canon', Marxist viii
capitalism 7–8, 11, 28, 34–6, 37, 44, 48–9, 63, 67
Catholicism xi, 18, 32–3, 34, 38, 53, 55–6, 60, 64
China 5
Christendom 23, 53
Christy, Henry 27
class struggle 7, 17, 56
Cohn, Norman 24
colonialism 6, 64
 neo-colonialism 53
Comte, Auguste viii, 11–13

communes xi
communism 23, 33, 38
 pre-Marxist x–xi
Communist Manifesto, The 1–2, 4, 10–11, 17, 21
critical theory 45–6, 50, 65
cyborgs 47

dehumanisation 8, 65
Democritus 3
Denver, USA 47
Destutt, Antoine 16
detachment, value-free 51
diversity, religious ix
Dühring, Eugen von 24
eco-theologies 56, 61
egoism 2, 48, 67
Engels, Friedrich vii, viii, ix, x, 1, 2, 4, 11, 16, 20–30, 63
 Anti-Dühring 21, 24
 Letters from Wuppertal 22
 Ludwig Feuerbach and the End of Classical German Philosophy 21, 26

77

Peasant War in Germany, The 21, 23–4
Enlightenment 5, 47, 48
evangelization 52, 55–6, 64
evolution, historical 29
evolution, religious 24–5, 27, 28
fascism 32
feminism viii, 47, 60
fetishism 11, 13, 26, 28
feudalism 34–5, 67
Feuerbach, Ludwig 4, 7–8, 9, 11, 13, 22, 32, 63, 65
Fourier, Charles x, xi
France 10, 4, 57
Frankfurt School 43–51, 64, 65
Frankfurt, Germany 43
freedom 2, 5, 6, 39, 44, 46
Freire, Paolo 57–8
Freud, Sigmund vii, 44
functionalism viii, 37, 55
fundamentalism, religious 50

Gebara, Ivone 57, 60
Geneva, Switzerland 43, 58
geology 21
German Ideology, The 4, 16, 21
Germany 3, 4, 5, 22, 23, 38, 42, 43, 46
Gramsci, Antonio vii, 18, 32–40, 64, 66
Greeks, ancient 3, 5
Grünberg, Carl 43
Gutierrez, Gustavo 57–8

Habermas, Jürgen 45–51, 67
Hall, Stuart viii, 37, 39–41
Haraway, Donna vii, 47
Hegel, Georg Wilhelm Friedrich 4–7, 9, 13, 32, 65
Lectures on the Philosophy of History 5
Hegelianism 9
Hegelians, Young 3, 4, 22
hegemony 36, 38–9, 40, 66
Heidegger, Martin 47

Index

Hennequin, Victor x–xi
Hinduism ix
history viii, 1, 25, 27,
   29, 56, 66
   Marxist 17, 23, 44
   world 5–6, 7, 9
Hobsbawm, Eric 24
Horkheimer, Max 43,
   45–7, 50

Ibn Khaldun 12
Icarians xi
ideology x, 9, 12, 15–17,
   19, 32–4, 36–7, 40,
   43, 56, 66, 68
inclusivity 56, 61
India 5
institutions, religious ix,
   x, 3, 23, 33, 34, 37,
   38, 53, 63
Islam ix
Italy 32–3, 38

journalism 4
Judaism ix, 3, 45

L'Atelier (newspaper) xi
Labayen, bishop 53
labour 7, 8, 65
Laclau, Ernesto 33, 39
Lamennais, Felicité x

language, use of 13–14
Latin America 52–3, 55,
   57
Liberation Theology vii,
   52–61, 64
lifeworld, concept of 45,
   48–9, 67
linguistics 48, 50
lived religion viii–ix, 59
logic, dialectic 7
London, UK 4, 22
Luther, Martin 18
Maduro, Otto 57–9
Manchester, UK 22
Maoism 45
Marcuse, Herbert 44
Marx, Karl, life of ix, 1,
   3–4
   Capital 4, 10–11, 21,
      28
   *Communist Manifesto,
      The* see *Communist
      Manifesto, The*
   *Contribution to a
      Critique of Hegel's
      Philosophy of Right*
      10–11
   *Contribution to a
      Critique of Political
      Economy* 4, 9–11,
      14, 18, 33

79

Theses on Feuerbach
   8, 10–11
marxisms
   complexity of viii, xi
   'scientific' viii, 39
   variety of xi
   'without guarantees'
      viii, 33
   see also post-marxism
materialism 9, 12, 46, 56
Mexico 27
mill-owners 22
minorities, religious 3
modernity viii, 2, 6, 44, 49–50
monarchy x, 24, 35
monotheism ix, 26
Mouffe, Chantal 39
Münzer, Thomas 23–4
Mussolini, Benito 32

Nazism 43, 46–7
New York, USA 43

Oxford, University of 27
orientalism viii, 6, 55

Paris, France 4, 22, 47
parties, Communist 32
patriarchy 60

Pentecostalism 55
Persia 5
Philippines 53, 55
physiology 21
pluralism 50, 59
position, war of 38
positivism 12
post-marxism 33
power, constructions of viii, 3, 24, 33, 37–8, 55
production 2, 6
   forces of 9, 16, 66, 68
   mass 15
   mode of 6, 66, 67, 68
   of knowledge 17
   relations of 9, 14, 18, 66
proletariat 7
prosperity gospel 56
Protestantism ix, 22, 25
psychoanalysis viii, 44

Quakers 27

Rastafarianism ix
rationality 5, 12, 35, 44, 47–50, 67
reductionism 3, 67
Reformation 5, 18, 23, 25, 35, 44

Index

revolution x, 14, 23–4, 38, 63
Revolution, French x, 5, 12, 35
Revolution, Industrial 15
Ricoeur, Paul 60
ritual 34, 37
Russia 38

Saint Simon, Henri x, 12
Sardinia 32
schools 34–5, 38, 55
science 12, 16, 21, 26, 29, 47, 49, 66
social 45, 63
Scientology ix
secularization viii, 29, 48, 59
sex 44–5, 6
slavery 5, 6
socialism x, xi, 47
sociology vii–viii, ix, 1, 2, 9, 11, 12, 14, 21, 32, 35, 37, 43, 44, 45, 48, 50, 55, 66
 of religion viii, 25, 29, 51, 58–9, 63

soul 26, 34
Soviet Union 43, 46
species-being 8, 27
spiritualities, alternative 29
Stalin, Joseph 46
State Apparatuses, Ideological (ISAs) 32, 34
Stuttgart, Germany 5, 15
superstructure, ideological 9, 13–19, 33, 37, 39–40, 66, 68
technologies 14, 27, 66
totemism 26
Trier, Germany 3
Tylor, Edward B. vii, 24, 26–30
uncertainty 2, 12, 39, 41
Vatican II 53
Venezuela 58
Weber, Max vii, 44, 55
Weil, Felix 42
working class xi, 22
World Council of Churches 58
Worsley, Peter 24
yoga, tantric 45

www.ingramcontent.com/pod-product-compliance
Lightning Source LLC
Chambersburg PA
CBHW042141160426
43201CB00021B/2365